FINISHED THINGS

Chasing the Other Side of Done

EDWARD BEALE

and

WILLIAM PARRY

Edward Beale with William Parry

FINISHED THINGS is a work of nonfiction.
www.expeditionaire.com
9 8 7 6 5 4 3 2 1
SECOND EDITION

Book editing and design by Edward K. Beale.

Published in the United States of America.
Library of Congress Control Number: 2025914552
Self-Published by Expeditionaire
East Brookfield, Massachusetts, USA.
/ finished things: chasing the other side of done /
/ Edward Beale William Parry /
1. Nonfiction / Business
2. Nonfiction / Self Help
25.07.25
ISBN: 0-9976601-3-5
ISBN-13: 978-0-9976601-3-5

DEDICATION

For Michelle, Christine, and Hilary,
who lived with the unfinished things on this side of done
for too many years.

Table of Contents

INTRODUCTION

Somewhere Between "Start" and "Done"

It started, as so many things do, with a message that wasn't supposed to be profound.

"Well, it isn't *not* moving. But it also isn't *done.*"

This was written half in jest during one of our daily check-ins. It was about a project that had been.... lingering. You know the kind. It had a name, a folder, a few hundred brilliant ideas - and zero forward momentum.

We laughed, because it was true. We groaned, because it was familiar.

And then we paused.

Because that single sentence summed up what we've seen in ourselves, our peers, and people all over the working world: **stuck between the excitement of beginning and the clarity of finishing**. Somewhere in the middle. Somewhere in the fog, working on a thing that isn't quite dead, but isn't quite moving either.

Welcome to the gap on *this* side of done.

We've lived there. Sat with it, fought through it, talked it to death. Back and forth. Every. Single. Day. For. Years. We got stuck in that uncomfortable middle.

So, here's what we talked about, distilled into the book we should have had back then. It's our private struggle written for you, still stumbling along on the road to the other side of *done*. The place we all want to be. The place of Finished Things.

Done is a Place

Every professional knows the weight of things undone. The email left unsent. The slide deck not quite ready. The book idea still sitting in a notes app.

We imagine that one day we'll wake up with perfect clarity, ample time, a clear schedule, and ideal energy. Then, finally, we'll finish what we started.

That day never comes.

The Other Side of Done is not a fantasy. It's a place. It's real. And it's reachable, but only if we change our thinking.

We've spent decades helping others cross the finish line. We've also spent weeks spinning our wheels. We've delivered on massive projects and abandoned personal goals.

This book is everything we've learned about what works. It's for anyone who's tired of being "almost there." It's practical. It's positive. It's blunt.

It's for you.

A Pep Talk? OK.

But a pep talk will not get it done.

Let's be clear.

This isn't another motivational book that tells you to chase your dreams and hustle until your eyeballs bleed. You won't find any hype here. No "10x hacks." No forced positivity. No diagrams that pretend execution is a clean, upward curve.

You'll find something more useful: **truth**.

Not the kind you put on a coffee mug. The kind you learn at 2 a.m. on a deadline, when your imposter syndrome is louder than your team chat. The kind you figure out after shipping something ugly, and realize it still moved the needle.

We wrote *Finished Things* because we've been in the trenches. We know what it's like to wrestle a good idea and chase it all the way to the other side of done. We know how hard it is to finish something when your energy is low, your inbox is full, and your inner critic won't shut up.

We've also learned this: **done is always worth it**.

What's In It for You?

This book is short on fluff and long on real. Each chapter tackles a piece of the process that nobody warns you about: resistance, shame, routine, debt, burnout, feedback, imperfection - and offers one thing most books forget:

Permission to finish anyway.

Grab a highlighter, grab a pen. Read through, take notes, complete the actions steps. The finish line is right over there.

We'll help you:

Start even when you can't see the finish.

Build small, repeatable habits instead of chasing unicorns.

Make peace with messy progress.

Stay in motion through hard seasons.

Ship before you're ready.

Trust yourself again.

And maybe, just maybe, laugh a little along the way.

Because let's be honest: some days, the best you can do is open the file, stare at it for five minutes, and move one block of text. That still counts. You're still in the game.

And if you keep going, one day, not long from now, you'll look up and realize:

"I'm on the other side of done. I have a Finished Thing."

We hope this book helps you get there.

Let's go.

- **Ed & Bill**

Edward Beale with William Parry

Chapter 1

YOU CAN'T SEE DONE FROM HERE

"Done" is seductive. It glows on the horizon like a lighthouse on a stormy coast: steady, reassuring, and just out of reach. From the starting line, we fantasize about what "done" will feel like. Accomplishment. Clarity. Relief. Respect.

But here's the truth: at the beginning, you can't see done. Not clearly. Not even vaguely.

And that's where most people stall.

They confuse not seeing the path with there being no path. They wait for clarity. They wait for motivation. They wait for the clouds to part. But starting isn't about having all the answers. It's about taking the first step anyway.

Clarity doesn't come before action. It comes *because of* action.

You don't need a ten-year plan. You don't need another certification. You don't need to journal your way to enlightenment. What you need is to move. Because motion builds momentum, and momentum reveals direction.

The Start is the Scariest Part

Everyone wants the finish line. Everyone gets the middle. But the start? The start feels like standing on the edge of a high dive with no water in the pool below. It's raw. It's lonely. And it's easy to talk yourself out of jumping.

That's where people stay stuck. Not because they're lazy, but because they're scared. Scared to look foolish. Scared to be wrong. Scared to waste time.

That fear doesn't go away. You just learn to act in spite of it.

Waiting is a Trap

Too many smart people are stuck in what we call the "Perfection Trap."

Here's how it happens:

You start a project. You get excited. Then you think, "This *has* to be amazing."

So you tweak. And polish. And restart. And doubt yourself.

And nothing ships. You're waiting for the perfect time.

The "perfect time" is a myth. Conditions will never be ideal. Your inbox will never be empty. Your energy will never be perfect. And yes, someone will always have it more figured out than you.

Waiting for the perfect time is really just procrastination in a nicer outfit.

If you've had an idea in your head for more than 30 days and haven't made a move, you're not waiting - you're avoiding.

Finished projects can be improved. But unfinished ones can't even be used.

Here's the truth: most people don't need your perfect. They need your finished.

What to Do When You're Stuck

We all get stuck. Here's our reboot checklist:

- Move your body. Walk. Stretch. Get blood flowing.
- Change your environment. New room, coffee shop, anything.
- Do a 10-minute timer challenge: "What can I do in 10 minutes?"
- Text someone. Ask for accountability.
- Finish something small: a file, a call, a note.

Momentum often comes after motion.

Get Moving. Now.

Start where you are. Use what you have. Do what you can.

You don't need a whiteboard session. You need a notebook and a first task.

You don't need a new website. You need a working draft.

You don't need a new you. You need to work with the one that's already here.

Because the 'you' that gets to "done" will be shaped by the doing.

Truth Check

- You can't think your way to "done."
- You can't plan your way to "done."
- You have to *do your way* to "done."

No one else is going to start for you. And no one else can feel what it's like when you finally make it through.

So get uncomfortable. Get scrappy. Start ugly.

Just start.

Action Step

Write down the project you keep putting off. Then write the next smallest physical action you can take in the next 15 minutes. Now do it, just that one thing. No perfection. No delay. Just do.

Edward Beale with William Parry

J. K. Rowling (Author)

When Rowling began *Harry Potter and the Philosopher's Stone*, she famously didn't know how the series would end - she carried only a handful of chapter ideas and character sketches. Instead of waiting for perfect clarity, she let inspiration drive the story's direction with each draft. This page-by-page discovery yielded plot threads and character arcs she couldn't have planned. Her "snowball writing" approach, where the momentum of daily writing reveals the shape of the end, mirrors the chapter's core lesson: **clarity comes from action, not foresight.**

George R. R. Martin (Author)

George R. R. Martin began *A Game of Thrones* in with a single vivid scene: an unnamed boy watching a man's execution in the snow. In interviews, Martin has described himself as a "gardener, not an architect" who plants characters and follows where they grow. His open-ended approach means he often can't see the full story arc from the beginning, but he keeps moving forward scene by scene. Martin has built an intricately detailed world by trusting that momentum reveals direction. His career proves that **starting without a map is how some of the most beloved stories in modern fiction come to life.**

Edward Beale with William Parry

Chapter 2

THE IDEA ISN'T THE HARD PART

✧

Ideas are easy.

They show up in the shower, and during your walk, and again right before you fall asleep. You get excited, scribble notes, maybe even tell a friend. It feels like progress.

But it's not.

An idea is nothing until you act on it. Like a workout, it means nothing until you break a sweat. Nothing - until *something* exists in the world that didn't before.

We live in an era that worships "the idea", where people are rewarded for pitch decks, not products. The vision gets the likes and shares, never the execution. But vision without action is just hallucination. An idea without a deadline is just a dream.

The Seduction of Potential

It feels better to dream than to build.

Dreaming is clean. Infinite. Safe.

But dreaming doesn't put anything in the world.

Building is gritty. It's late nights, missed calls, and more edits than you thought humanly possible. The people who win are not the ones with the best ideas. They're the ones who act on *good-enough* ideas with relentless execution.

We've met plenty of smart people who never shipped. We've also met average thinkers who became exceptional doers - and they took it past the finish line.

You're Not Waiting on Inspiration. You're Avoiding Accountability.

If you say you're "not ready" yet, ask this: **what are you really avoiding?**

Is it criticism? Is it failure? Is it responsibility?

That's the real reason most ideas die in notebooks. There's no risk in a concept. No rejection in a draft. No failure in a someday.

But the longer you sit on an idea, the heavier it gets. Eventually it turns into shame. The idea becomes a symbol, not of possibility, but of avoidance.

So what's the solution? It's one word: Ship.

Perfect < Done

Here's an oldie but a goodie: "Perfection is where creativity goes to die."

If your first version doesn't embarrass you at least a little, you waited too long. Don't aim for perfection. Aim for something you can test, touch, and improve.

Done lets you iterate. Done lets you learn. Done lets you start over again on something else and get even better.

The perfect idea that never shipped will always lose to the imperfect product that did.

Be the One Who Finishes

Ideas are everywhere. Finishers are rare.

What's the difference? Follow-through.

We've coached leaders with billion-dollar visions who couldn't execute a five-page memo.

We've also worked with quiet interns who launched entire campaigns.

Finishers:

- Set deadlines.
- Honor them.
- Learn from misses without quitting.

Start Small, But Start Now

Write the blog post, even if no one reads it.

Record the first podcast, even if the audio sucks.

Launch the offer, even if only one person buys.

START - HONE - ITERATE - PUSH it (out into the world.) S.H.I.P. that thing.

You don't need mass approval. You need movement, not the applause of strangers. Execution is feedback, if you're paying attention. And feedback makes you better, if you care.

We know you do.

Action Step

Pick one idea that's been living in your head. Set a 30-minute timer. Do the roughest, fastest version of that idea you can. Sketch it. Write it. Record it. Build it. Send it. Just ship *something*. Today.

Edward Beale with William Parry

14

LIN-MANUEL MIRANDA (PLAYWRIGHT & COMPOSER)

Lin-Manuel Miranda conceived *Hamilton* on a flight, scribbling rap lyrics in a notebook. He committed to writing and sharing incomplete versions, performing rough drafts at workshops, soliciting feedback, and iterating weekly. Instead of perfecting every lyric in isolation, he "shipped" partial versions to live audiences, learning what resonated. That willingness to release an unfinished work, absorb real-time reactions, and continuously refine embodies the advice: **ideas are plentiful - shipping is the real art.**

WALT DISNEY (ANIMATOR & ENTREPRENEUR)

When Walt Disney first dreamed up Mickey Mouse in 1928, it was only a rough sketch and a charming concept. Yet *Steamboat Willie* nearly broke him. Disney treated the film as a "rough prototype", staging a makeshift screening with pots, pans, harmonicas, and live Foley effects to test timing and audience reaction. The test audience's rapturous response helped him push ahead for a national release. Shipping the first "good-enough" version brought real feedback and rapid iteration. Disney's leap from concept to execution teaches that **ideas are cheap; shipping something - even imperfect - is where the true creative work begins.**

Edward Beale with William Parry

Chapter 3

ROUTINE BUILDS MOMENTUM

⋎

Motivation is unreliable.

You can't wait for it or force it. And when you do have it, it usually fades just when you need it most. That's why professionals don't depend on motivation. They build routines.

Routine is what gets you through the days you don't feel like doing the work. And there will be plenty of those.

If motivation is the spark, routine is the engine.

It's Always About Energy

You can have 8 hours free and still get nothing done.

Why? Because *energy* is the *real* currency of productivity.

You can't fake energy. You can't "wish it into being." But you can design for it.

We've learned to ask: What fuels me? What drains me? Then we engineer our days around those answers.

Energy truths:

- Sleep is a productivity tool.

- Movement fuels focus.

- Emotional health affects creative output.

Start your day with a 10-minute win, something small but meaningful. It generates momentum, movement, energy in the direction of DONE.

Energy Follows Structure

You don't look like your goals; you look like your habits.

Fix your habits to reach your goals. The hardest part is getting started. Every single day.

That's why you need *scaffolding*, some *structure* to hold you up while the internal engine sputters into gear. Left to chance, your energy will drift. Structure gives it a channel.

Routines create rhythm, rhythm leads to progress, progress generates momentum, and momentum sustains itself.

This is why world-class performers, from athletes to CEOs, don't wing it. They schedule everything. They stack habits. They automate their discipline.

And when life gets chaotic? Routine becomes the rope that pulls them through.

Don't Overcomplicate It

People often imagine routine as a full-blown productivity system with color-coded calendars and bulletproof to-do lists.

That's a trap.

A good routine doesn't need to be fancy. It just needs to be repeatable.

- Wake up at the same time.
- Drink a glass of water.
- Write for 20 minutes.
- Go for a walk.
- Make your bed.
- Open your work doc and start typing.

One or two consistent actions, done every day, build a groove. And in that groove, the work gets easier. You become like a bobsled in a track and the speed is inevitable.

You don't have to reinvent yourself. You just need to show up the same way, again and again.

The Body Leads the Mind

If your energy is garbage, your execution will be too. Start there.

Move your body. Lift something heavy. Get out in the sun. Take your vitamins. Drink more water. Eat food that didn't come out of a wrapper.

This isn't new advice. It's just ignored because it's boring. But your physical energy is the fuel for your mental stamina. No energy, no focus. No focus, no done.

So treat your body like the vehicle it is. You don't have to turn into a health nut. But you do have to stop pretending burnout is a badge of honor.

You're not a machine, except for this one same thing - you do need good maintenance.

Routine Kills Resistance

When something is part of your routine, it's no longer a debate.

You don't think about brushing your teeth. You just do it.

You can make writing that daily paragraph just as automatic. Or reviewing that one spreadsheet. Or emailing your key client. Or building whatever habit gets you to done.

Once something is part of your routine, resistance loses its grip.

And the days you miss? Don't spiral. Just pick up where you left off.

Consistency isn't about never falling. It's about always coming back.

Your Calendar Is a Mirror

We hear this all the time: "I just don't have time." But time isn't the issue. Prioritization is.

If we audited your calendar, we'd see exactly what you value. Meetings with others? Always there. Deep work time for your big goals? Usually missing.

That's because we prioritize others' needs over our own progress.

Reclaim your calendar. Block time for what matters.

Try this:

- Create a daily 90-minute "Focus Slot."
- Use it for the one thing that moves your most important project forward.
- No email. No meetings. No "quick questions."

"If it matters, it must be scheduled."

Edward Beale with William Parry

Action Step

Choose one small task that moves your project forward.
Schedule it at the same time every day for one week.
Use an alarm if you have to. Don't aim for perfect - just
aim to get a little closer to a finished thing each day.
Build the muscle.

Edward Beale with William Parry

ERNEST HEMINGWAY (NOVELIST)

Ernest Hemingway famously made writing a daily appointment. As he told George Plimpton, "When I am working on a book or a story, I write every morning as soon after first light as possible. There is no one to disturb you, and [you] write until you come to a place where you [...] know what will happen next." By showing up every dawn, no matter his mood or inspiration, Hemingway built unstoppable momentum. His strict morning routine carried him through classics like *The Sun Also Rises* and *A Farewell to Arms*, proving that **consistency, not bursts of motivation, propels you across the finish line.**

STEPHEN KING (NOVELIST)

King credits his astonishing output - over 60 novels - to a simple daily routine: writing 2,000 words every morning, seven days a week, no exceptions. On weekends, holidays, even birthdays, he sits at his desk and dutifully types until the quota is met. This reliable practice produces drafts that keep moving forward, whether he "feels motivated" or not. Over decades, that unglamorous habit has yielded classics like *The Shining* and *It*. King's example proves that **routine, not inspiration, is the engine of completion.**

Edward Beale with William Parry

Chapter 4

DECLUTTER OR DIE

✣

Clutter kills clarity.

It slows you down, clouds your thinking, and eats away at your energy. Whether it's your desk, your inbox, or your head, clutter is friction, and friction is the enemy of getting things done.

If you're serious about finishing, you're going to have to clear the decks.

Noise is the New Normal

We live surrounded by noise: notifications, opinions, distractions, open tabs, half-finished ideas. Most of it isn't urgent, but it all demands your attention, and none of it moves the needle.

That's the problem.

You can't do deep work in a shallow environment. You can't find the path when you're ankle-deep in mess.

So clear it.

Simplify your space. Simplify your tools. Simplify your process. If it doesn't help you ship, get rid of it.

Clarity is a Byproduct of Simplicity

Don't confuse complexity with sophistication. Real pros don't complicate things, they streamline them.

- One notebook.
- One system.
- One goal at a time.

That's how things get finished.

If your project is stalled, ask yourself: what's in the way? Is it a decision you've avoided? A task you keep moving down the list? A drawer you never opened?

Whatever it is, clean it out.

You don't need to organize everything. You need to remove what doesn't serve the work.

Simplicity Wins. Always.

We once reviewed a 93-slide pitch deck. The CEO wanted feedback. Our advice?

"Turn it into 10 slides. Then 6. Then 1."

The audience isn't looking for complexity. They want clarity.

Whether it's a strategy doc, an onboarding process, or a marketing funnel, simplify it until it sings.

Start with:

- What is the one thing this "Finished Thing" must achieve?

- What can be cut without losing meaning?

- What would make this faster to understand?

Then do it.

Your Focus Determines Your Reality

Anakin Skywalker got that gem of a lesson from Master Qui-Gon Jin. As an only child on a desert planet, a tinkering mechanic with a half-finished protocol droid and a wonky podracer, and the shopkeeping slave for a barely understandable parts merchant, his life was a total mess.

But Anakin's master got him to focus on one finished thing first: win the pod race.

Then the next finished thing: become a Jedi.

The Tools Don't Matter. The Work Does.

We've used fancy editing software and handwritten notes on napkins.

What matters is not the platform.

It's the process and the progress.

If you find yourself switching tools often, ask: "Am I optimizing for results or avoiding the work?"

Our advice:

- Pick one tool. Stick with it for 30 days.
- Focus on learning the 80% that gets you results.
- Ignore features you don't need (for now).

Emotional Clutter is Real

It's not just your environment, it's your inner dialogue. The guilt, the doubt, the past failures whispering in your ear. Those count as clutter too.

And the longer you leave them unchecked, the more space they take up.

You can't outwork a mental loop that says, "you're not good enough." You have to interrupt it. Replace it. Or simply acknowledge it and do the work anyway.

Sometimes the most powerful thing you can do is forgive yourself for not being further along.

Then get back to *move*.

Time Clutter is Real

They say corporate culture is not what you feel on Monday morning. It's what you feel on Sunday night.

The dread of going back to work can be a huge anchor on your progress. You can't make a dent in *done* if you hate the idea of going to the office.

That "anxiety clock" ticking in the back of your mind is "time clutter."

Daily commute got you down? Leave earlier.

The threat of an early alarm keeping you awake all night? Fix the pre-sleep routine.

Depressed at the thought of walking into a chaotic workspace? Take 15 minutes and set tomorrow's stage at the end of each day.

(This is absolutely a great life hack if you can make it a habit. Starting with a clear palette and everything already laid out jumpstarts momentum towards the finish.)

The clock and calendar might be crushing the spark during your down time. Don't let them. Leave work at work. Slay the time clutter. Compartmentalize.

Build with Less

Constraints are not the enemy, they're a gift.

You'll be amazed what you can build with fewer tools, fewer meetings, fewer steps.

Complexity is often just procrastination dressed in process.

Try doing more with less:

- Fewer meetings, more decision-making.
- Fewer drafts, more publishing.
- Fewer collaborators, more ownership.

Done loves simplicity.

Action Step

Pick one physical (or temporal, or metaphorical) space to declutter today, the one that keeps tripping up your progress. Maybe your desktop. Your to-do list. Your calendar. Or even your head. Eliminate five things that don't serve the goal. Then use that reclaimed space to take the next step.

Edward Beale with William Parry

MICHELANGELO (SCULPTOR & PAINTER)

When carving his Pietà and later David, Michelangelo famously spoke of freeing the figure trapped in the marble. He began by stripping away all excess stone, literally decluttering his medium, until only the completed form remained. In his workshop, excess chips and discarded chunks were swept away to keep the focus squarely on the emerging sculpture. By clearing away every distraction from his workspace and his mind, he exemplified the chapter's tenet: **simplicity and focus are prerequisites for finishing great work.**

STEVE JOBS (TECH VISIONARY)

When Steve Jobs returned to Apple in 1997, he found a bewildering array of over a dozen Mac models, and countless peripherals, confusing customers and bleeding the company dry. Rather than add more features or products, he grabbed a marker, drew a simple 2×2 grid on a whiteboard, and declared that Apple would focus on just four machines (consumer/pro desktop, and consumer/pro portable), shelving everything else. Within a year, Apple swung from a billion-dollar loss to a $309 million profit. By ruthlessly cutting "the noise" and streamlining to its core offerings, Jobs proved that **finishing great work often begins by eliminating everything that distracts you.**

Edward Beale with William Parry

Chapter 5

TEAM BEATS TALENT

ⵦ

Talent is overrated.

It's not who's smartest or fastest. It's who can stay in the game long enough to finish: the Tortoise, not the Hare. And the people who stay in the game usually aren't doing it alone.

If you want to reach "done," you're going to need a team. Not necessarily employees. Not necessarily co-founders. But people. Support. Accountability. Perspective.

Even a solo journey has a group effort behind the scenes.

Lone Wolves Burn Out

Working alone can feel noble and rugged. Heroic even.

It also gets lonely. Fast.

When you're isolated, the smallest challenge becomes overwhelming. The highs don't feel as high, and the lows hit harder. One tough day can take you out of the game for weeks.

This isn't weakness. It's just how humans work. To help fight this, we are wired for connection.

Collaboration isn't a luxury - it's a survival strategy.

You don't need a hundred people. You just need a few who get it. People who show up, ask the right questions, challenge your blind spots, and pull you forward when you stall.

Coaches, Not Cheerleaders

Support doesn't mean endless encouragement.

In fact, what you need more than praise is perspective. Someone who will look you in the eye and say, "This is unclear" or "This is taking too long" or "You're capable of more."

That's what a coach does.

A coach doesn't do the work for you. A coach helps you see what you can't. They tighten your form. Shorten your path. Keep you accountable to your own potential.

That's the kind of voice you want in your corner. Not just someone to say, "you're doing great," but someone who can help you do better.

Put Down Your Bucket

There's a great story about a ship at sea, far from land. They ran out of water and signaled frantically for another ship to share even one barrel.

The reply?

"Put down your buckets where you are." Turns out they were at the mouth of the Amazon River, surrounded by fresh water.

The team you need is all around you.

Your neighbor might know the way over the next hurdle. Your cousin knows a guy with the solution you need. Have you asked them? The fix might be a LinkedIn post away, a gift in comments from the hive mind.

Put down that bucket, and drink solutions with a team.

Your Circle Shapes Your Output

They say the five people you spend the most time with determine your direction.

The people around you are either pulling you toward done... or away from it.

Pay attention:

- Who challenges you to grow?
- Who distracts you from your priorities?

- Who believes in your goal, even when you stop believing in it?

Choose your inputs with intention. A good partner can accelerate your momentum. The wrong one will derail it.

This applies to friends, family, collaborators, mentors, and even your own inner circle of thoughts. Keep what helps. Exit what doesn't.

Don't Wait to Be Chosen

The biggest lie about teamwork is that it's something you wait for.

You don't have to wait for a coach to find you.

You don't need permission to build your own circle.

Honestly, those people need you as much as you need them.

Reach out. Ask for input. Offer to help first. Create the kind of collaboration you wish existed.

It's not about finding the "perfect" partner. It's about aligning with people who are headed in the same direction - and are willing to row.

You don't need to do this alone. And you shouldn't.

Accountability comes from the outside

It's a rare person who can crack the whip on themselves.

So hand the whip to a friend. A cheerleader. An accountability buddy.

Their one job is to yell at you.

They keep yelling this: "Do the thing!"

Because from the outside they can see what you're really doing.

And remind you that:

- Thinking about the thing - is not doing the thing.

- Talking about the thing - is not doing the thing.

- Buying gear for the thing - is not doing the thing.

- Doing another thing first - is not doing the thing.

"Do the thing!"

Edward Beale with William Parry

Action Step

Reach out to one person who can help move your project forward. Ask for their insight, feedback, or support. Set a time to check in. Accountability is a shortcut to "done."

Edward Beale with William Parry

THE BEATLES (SONGWRITERS & PERFORMERS)

Though Lennon and McCartney are celebrated songwriting geniuses, their best work often arose from collective studio sessions with George Harrison, Ringo Starr, producer George Martin, and engineers. On *Sgt. Pepper's Lonely Hearts Club Band*, suggestions from the group such as unexpected instruments, a revised harmony, a fresh lyrical turn, all elevated individual ideas into enduring songs. Their collaborative model shows that **even icons rely on a tuned-in team to catch blind spots and push a project across the finish line.**

QUENTIN TARANTINO (FILMMAKER)

Quentin Tarantino's greatest successes have always been deeply collaborative. Early in his career, he struggled to translate his screenplays into finished films on his own. Then he found editor Sally Menke, who tightened his sprawling scripts into cinematic classics. like *Reservoir Dogs* and *Inglourious Basterds*. His recurring partnerships with actors like Uma Thurman, cinematographers like Robert Richardson, and producers like Lawrence Bender helped transform raw ideas into polished, enduring works. Tarantino's journey proves the chapter's lesson: **even the most talented creators reach their full potential when they trust and depend on a skilled, honest, invested team.**

Edward Beale with William Parry

Chapter 6

PROGRESS IS UGLY

꙳

There's a myth that success looks clean. That the path to *done* is organized, well-lit, and steadily uphill.

It's not.

Progress is messy. It's nonlinear and frustrating. It's late nights, false starts, and that sinking feeling when you realize you've built something that needs to be rebuilt.

Ugly is normal.

If your process looks like a beautiful Instagram post, you're probably not doing the real work yet.

Expect the Swamp

Every meaningful project hits the swamp, that thick, unglamorous middle where nothing seems to move and everything feels like a mistake.

You'll wonder why you started.

You'll think you're not good enough.

You'll be tempted to quit.

You'll fantasize about a new idea, because the new one always looks cleaner, simpler, easier.

Don't fall for it.

The swamp isn't a signal to stop. It's a signal that you're doing something real. This is where the transformation happens - between the excitement of starting and the relief of finishing.

You want results? Learn to love the swamp.

Version One Is Supposed to Suck

Of course that first cut sucks! Nobody nails it the first time.

The draft will be rough. The prototype will break. The campaign will underperform. That doesn't mean you failed. Not even close. It means you started.

Too many people stop at the first ugly outcome. They take early imperfection as a final verdict. It's not. It's a beginning.

Give yourself permission to suck. Give yourself permission to keep going anyway.

Because beneath the ugly is progress in disguise, the unpainted scaffolding of *done*.

Public Work, Private Struggle

What you see online is the highlight reel. What gets you to *done* is the behind-the-scenes grind nobody shows.

You don't see:

- The edits that got deleted.
- The conversations that got heated.
- The tears, the caffeine, the self-doubt.

But they're always there.

The people who finish learn to *carry the chaos* without letting it define them. They learn to keep going, even when the process feels like a train wreck.

It's not about how it looks. It's about whether it moves you forward.

The Power of a Prototype

No prototype, no grade. You don't deserve one. You haven't turned anything in yet!

There's nothing - NOTHING - like holding a proof copy of your next book, or an unpainted 3D print of your new gizmet, or a working model of yesterday's plans.

Because they're real things. Not finished things, sure.

But a prototype lets you do two things: 1) see the other side of done, and 2) see how far you have to go.

A prototype is tangible, quantifiable, *something*. You can give a grade to it, and say - yeah, that's a solid "B minus."

With a prototype you'll know how much one costs, how heavy it is, how it sits on the shelf with your other Finished Things.

You can show it to friends.

Even better, you can show it to customers and investors.

You can share a dream that's been made REAL. The finish line, the final grade, is just beyond this prototype. It's proof you CAN make something real. Proof for *them*. Most important, proof for *yourself.*

Start Ugly, Stay Honest, Ship Anyway

Progress isn't pretty. But an ugly freight train doesn't need to be pretty to be powerful.

If you're in the middle and it feels like a mess, congratulations. You're doing it right! Just don't stop. Refine. Iterate. Keep building.

Finish the ugly version. Ship the imperfect product. Move forward.

The only people who never feel embarrassed by their early work are the ones who never finished.

Action Step

Find one piece of your current work that feels unfinished or rough. Instead of fixing it, ship it - to a friend, a coach, a small group. Get feedback. Take notes. Make the next version better. Let ugly be your launch pad.

Edward Beale with William Parry

GEORGE LUCAS (FILMMAKER & SCREENWRITER)

When George Lucas first wrote *Star Wars*, his first thirteen-page treatment, scrawled by hand on notebook paper, was so muddled that his own agent "didn't understand a single word." For the next year, Lucas produced four major drafts while fighting crippling writer's block. Yet he refused to wait for "perfect", chipping away even after shooting began. "If I hadn't been forced to shoot the film, I would doubtless still be rewriting it now." Lucas embraced each ugly messy draft and shipped the world-launching epic we know today - proof that **moving through the mess is the only path to finishing something great.**

FRANK GEHRY (ARCHITECT)

Frank Gehry's signature swooping forms, like the Guggenheim Bilbao, Disney Concert Hall, all begin in glorious chaos. He starts with loose, dream-like sketches that become "squirrelly, scrap like" models. Then his team builds 50–60 iterations, discarding the stale and enlarging the promising bits. Hundreds of digital tweaks fix the structural wrinkles, like musicians riffing to find the melody. Rather than wait for a perfect concept, Gehry knows the mess teaches what works. His breakthrough buildings prove that **progress rarely looks beautiful at first - mastery emerges only by iterating through the ugly.**

Edward Beale with William Parry

Chapter 7

WHEN LIFE GETS IN THE WAY

✤

You will be interrupted.

You will lose momentum. You'll get sick. Someone you love will need you. A bill will come due. A job will fall through. You'll face heartbreak, exhaustion, grief, and just plain bad luck.

Life doesn't stop just because you started a project.

It piles on.

And here's the truth nobody says out loud: getting to the other side of "done" means learning how to keep going when nothing is going your way.

You're Not Broken. You're Human.

When life sideswipes your plans, it's easy to take it personally.

You'll start to wonder if you're just not cut out for this. You'll say things like:

- "I can't focus."

- "I'm too tired."
- "Maybe I'm just not built for this."

But it's not you. It's life.

And life doesn't care about your to-do list. It shows up on its own schedule. What matters isn't avoiding it. What matters is how you respond.

Do you shut down? Or do you find a way to take one step forward, even with a weight on your chest?

Survival Mode Is Not Forever

There are seasons when survival *is* the victory.

You're not lazy if you didn't finish your project while grieving.

You're not undisciplined if you didn't hit your targets while your life was falling apart.

Remember, you are not a machine. Hibernation gets the bear through a long cold winter. Then it warms up again and the bear is back.

Some seasons can be about keeping the lights on, just don't confuse a pause with a full stop.

We've had days where all we could do was update one file. Then that one file re-lit the fire.

Even in survival mode, you can move. Maybe slower. Maybe more gently. But forward. Always forward.

Breathe, Then Rebuild

When you're in the middle of chaos, go back to basics:

- Breathe. Literally. Get your nervous system under control.

- Eat something real. A snack bar is not real.

- Move your body. Even 15 minutes walking to the next block and back.

- Write down three things you're grateful for. Then write three more.

These are not productivity hacks. These are foundation repairs.

Then, once the fog starts to lift, give yourself some grace. Don't expect to jump back in at full speed. Start with one small task. One corner of the mess. One line on the page.

You don't need to feel 100% to make 1% progress. 1% per day means a Finished Thing on day 100.

Use the Pain

Some of the best work you'll ever do will be built from heartbreak.

That doesn't mean suffering is required. But the pain *can* be fuel. Pain gives you perspective. Loss clarifies what matters. Struggle strips away the nonessential.

So don't wait to be "fine." If you can't find motivation, work with what you've got. Use what you're feeling. Let it pour into the work. Put points on the board.

Make it all count.

Don't Try to Get Back to Normal. Build Forward

After a setback like burnout, layoffs, failure, or loss, we often try to "get back to normal."

But normal is gone.

The better strategy? Build something better. Move forward, not backward.

Ask yourself:

- What do I want more of in the next version of me?

- What do I want less of?

- What's one small step toward that today?

Change is hard. But rebuilding is possible.

"There is no going back. There is only building forward."

Action Step

Write down one thing that's weighing on you right now. Name it. Acknowledge it. Then write one thing you can do *today* that moves your project forward - despite it. Big goals survive on small wins during hard times.

Edward Beale with William Parry

PABLO PICASSO (PAINTER)

In early 1901, Pablo Picasso was rocked by the suicide of his close friend and fellow artist Carlos Casagemas. Poor, nearly starving, and wracked by grief, he could have abandoned his art. Instead, his famed Blue Period saw painting every single day, even when his hands shook. On poor-quality, reused canvases he created dozens of somber, monochromatic studies of society's outcasts. Each small painting was a step forward. Rather than wait for emotional "readiness," Picasso channeled personal tragedy into sustained creative motion. **When life intervenes, progress - even if messy and imperfect - is the path to completion.**

LUDWIG VAN BEETHOVEN (COMPOSER)

In his early thirties, Beethoven began losing his hearing - a devastating blow for a composer. He grappled with shame and despair, convinced his career was over. Yet rather than abandon his life's work, he adapted. He sketched melodies into notebooks and composed at a quieter pace. Those fragments coalesced into drafts of what would become the *Ninth Symphony*. Beethoven's approach of taking whatever small step he could, even under crushing circumstances, epitomizes the chapter's lesson: **you can keep moving forward, one note at a time, even when life feels unbearably hard.**

Edward Beale with William Parry

Chapter 8

MONEY TALKS, SHAME SCREAMS

✦

Money stress will sabotage your best work.

You can have a great idea, a clear plan, and the skills to pull it off - but if the money is tight and the pressure is high, you'll feel it in everything. Your creativity shrinks. Your confidence fades. Your decisions get reactive instead of strategic.

And the worst part? You don't just feel broke. You start to feel broken.

That's where shame creeps in. Most stalled projects hide behind shame. You feel behind. You missed deadlines. You're overwhelmed. So you avoid the work.

It's not because you're lazy. It's because shame blocks creativity.

Solution:

Forgive yourself. Literally say it: "I forgive myself for falling behind."

Restart with a clean slate and a small win.

Talk to someone safe.

Debt Is Heavy, Shame Is Heavier

Debt is a math problem. Shame is a prison.

Being behind on bills doesn't mean you're a failure. But it *feels* that way. And that feeling (left unchecked) will destroy your forward motion faster than any bill collector or market downturn.

Shame says:

- "You're falling behind."

- "You've made too many mistakes."

- "You have no business chasing your dream."

Shame turns practical problems into (perceived) personal attacks. It warps your identity. It tells you you're only worth what's in your bank account. And this brand of unchecked shame will not stop hammering - until you quit.

The only way out is to name it. Out loud. Without apology.

You are not your balance sheet.

You are not your debt.

You are not your mistakes.

Make the Money Plan Part of the Project

Money problems don't solve themselves. Avoidance just makes them louder.

So put your financial reality on paper, no matter how ugly it looks. Income, expenses, debts, assets. All of it.

Then make a plan, not a fantasy. A plan helps answer:

- What do you need to cut?
- What do you need to earn?
- What's the *minimum* viable version of your goal that still moves you forward?

This isn't about shrinking your dreams. It's about outsmarting your constraints.

Build the thing lean. Build it scrappy. Build it while you keep the lights on.

You don't need funding. You need follow-through.

Watch Who You're Listening To

There's no shortage of advice out there. Most of it comes from people who haven't done what you're trying to do.

Here's the rule: never take financial advice from someone who's bitter, broke, bored, or just trying to sell you something.

Surround yourself with people who are calm with money.

Not just rich - calm. There's a difference.

The people who've weathered storms can help you find a path. The people still caught in the storm will try to drown you in theirs.

Choose wisely.

Money Isn't the Goal - Freedom Is

Money is not the finish line. It's a tool. A lever. A way to buy time, space, and energy to do the things that matter.

So stop obsessing over six figures, seven figures, "passive income," or going viral. You don't need millions. You need margin, a buffer, some breathing room between your bills and your bandwidth.

The finish line is freedom, not just financially, but emotionally. The ability to wake up and do what you're here to do.

Money helps. But only if you keep it in its place.

Action Step

Take 30 minutes and write down your current financial reality. Then, write three actions you can take this week to reduce pressure: cut a cost, earn a little extra, or re-scope your project to fit your means. Shame dies in sunlight.

Edward Beale with William Parry

OPRAH WINFREY (MEDIA MOGUL)

Early in her career, Winfrey navigated profound financial hardship and the shame that came with it, working low-budget news jobs and living paycheck to paycheck. She began tracking every expense and negotiating incremental salary increases, turning transparency into leverage. As her revenue grew, she invested in her own production company, building a safety net that enabled creative risk. Oprah's journey illustrates how **naming financial reality and making pragmatic plans breaks the cycle of shame and fuels progress.**

ELTON JOHN (MUSICIAN & SONGWRITER)

At the height of his fame in the late 1980s, Elton John was living extravagantly, spending over £250,000 a month on shopping, property, parties, and a growing entourage. Despite massive record sales, he was in serious financial trouble. When his lifestyle caught up with him in 1990, he got sober, fixed his spending, and began to rebuild with clarity and purpose. He downsized, reorganized his finances, and took control of his business affairs. He also returned to work with renewed focus, and composed *The Lion King* soundtrack, a global success. He turned embarrassment into empowerment - proof that **you don't overcome financial chaos by hiding from it. You face the truth, forgive yourself, and move forward** - step by honest step.

Edward Beale with William Parry

Chapter 9

THE OTHER SIDE OF DONE

⭣

So what does *done* actually feel like?

Not like you think.

It's not a parade. It's not fireworks. It's not a standing ovation. More often than not, "done" feels quiet. Subtle. A mix of relief, exhaustion, and maybe even confusion.

It feels like this: *"That's it?"*

It also feels like: *"Everything just stopped moving."*

But don't let the stillness fool you. That quiet moment is power. Because once something is done - truly done - it can't be taken from you. It becomes part of who you are.

Done Changes You

Getting to the other side of done rewires your brain.

Having a Finished Thing is a superpower.

You've moved something from the world of intention to the world of reality. That's not just progress, it's proof.

Proof that you can finish. Proof that you can push through resistance. Proof that your ideas matter enough to exist in the real world.

This is how confidence is built, not through hype, but through completion.

Done builds trust in yourself.

Closure Beats Perfection

Most people don't lack ideas. They lack closure.

They bounce from draft to draft, project to project, chasing the high of "starting" and avoiding the discomfort of finishing. Why? Because finishing means it's real. Finishing invites feedback. Finishing ends the fantasy.

You can't build a legacy out of half-finished drafts.

You want momentum in your life? Start finishing things. Start drawing lines through the task list, making check marks in the margin. Start walking things across the finish line - even if they're messy.

Hacking a dirt path all the way through the jungle is better than paving a parking lot to nowhere.

Done is better than perfect, because done is repeatable.

Make Your Own Applause

Recognition is nice. But if you wait for it, you may be waiting a long time.

In many companies, praise is inconsistent or invisible. Great work happens silently.

That's why we teach people to **make their own applause**.

Here's how:

- Keep a personal win log. Every Friday, jot down one thing you did well.
- Save appreciative emails or texts.
- Share progress with trusted peers, not just managers.

Celebrate yourself - not out of ego, but out of momentum.

Mark the Moment

Don't just *cross* the finish line. *Notice it.*

Take a breath. Sit still. Capture how it feels.

Write it down. Record a voice memo. Take a photo. Do something – anything - to mark the shift from "not done" to "done." That moment matters.

Why? Because the next time you're stuck in the middle, you'll forget what finishing feels like. And you'll need a reminder that you've done this before, that you've crossed mountains. You know how to get to the other side. So celebrate.

Capture your wins. They will become your compass.

There's Always Another Side

"Done" isn't the end. It's the start of the next thing.

New ideas will come. New challenges will surface. But you'll face them differently now. Because you've been to the other side. And that changes how you move through the world.

Finishing something – anything - gives you a kind of internal armor. It doesn't make things easier. It makes *you* sturdier.

So celebrate. Rest. Recharge.

Then aim again out into the fog at the next future *Finished Thing*.

What do you see at the top of the mountain? Probably the next mountain. What a view!

Action Step

Choose one project you've completed, no matter how small. Write down how it made you feel. Capture what it taught you. Then write down one way you'll celebrate that win. This is how you build a history of momentum: one mountain top, one finish line at a time.

Edward Beale with William Parry

J. R. R. Tolkien (Author)

After decades of drafting and world-building, Tolkien finally completed *The Lord of the Rings*. When he handed in the manuscript, he expected thunderous acclaim, but instead found a quiet sense of relief. There was no grand parade, only the profound satisfaction of having moved his epic from imagination into reality. That understated closure perfectly captures this insight: **the finish line often feels quiet, but its power lies in irreversible creation.**

Michael Phelps (Swimmer)

After winning a record-breaking eight gold medals at the 2008 Beijing Olympics, Michael Phelps didn't celebrate with lavish parties. Instead, he took a solitary moment on the pool deck to remove his goggles, breathe deeply, and write in a small notebook: the exact times of each race, his feelings in the water, and one lesson learned per event. That ritual of marking the moment gave Phelps a tangible reminder of peak performance and its emotional texture. In the years that followed, he revisited those notes before every major competition, using them as a compass for training and mindset. By taking time to quietly honor "done," Phelps learned to **turn each (Olympic) victory into the foundation for the next pursuit.**

Edward Beale with William Parry

Chapter 10

ITERATE FOR EFFECT

❧

Done is not the end. It's the beginning of better.

Finishing something doesn't mean it's perfect. It means it's alive. It means it exists. And once it exists, you can improve it.

That's how real success works. Not through one-shot brilliance, but through steady iteration.

Launch. Learn. Adjust. Repeat.

This is the game. Iteration makes it a winnable game.

Version One Is Never the Final Version

Your first product will need fixes. Your first article will need edits. Your first launch will leave money on the table.

Good.

Because now you have feedback. You have data. You have momentum. You're no longer guessing - you're learning, improving.

The worst mistake you can make after finishing something is to stop working on it. The best move? Make the next better version.

The Second Coat Is Usually Easier

Every painter loves the second coat.

That first coat of paint? It's never exactly right. There's always a streak or a drip or some of the old color showing through. Sure it's "done" but, well, *really*?

But the second coat – that's where the magic happens.

It takes less "paint": less time, less brainpower, less *everything* to roll out a better finish.

After a second coat, the wall is "even more finished." If anything, the second version is where you wanted to be during the "dream" stage.

Grab that brush.

Systems, Not One-Offs

Professionals don't aim to create something once. They aim to create something repeatable.

They build systems. Templates. Checklists. Workflows. They make the process easier to replicate, scale, and improve.

Because when you're stuck in one-off mode, everything is harder than it has to be. You burn energy reinventing the wheel every time.

Want to free yourself up? Systematize.

- What worked? Capture it.
- What didn't? Fix it.
- What surprised you? Plan for it next time.

That's how "good" turns into "great."

Don't Burn It All Down, Shine It Up

You're allowed to revise without shame.

So many people get embarrassed by their early work. They want to hide it or delete it or pretend it never happened.

Don't.

Keep it up. Let people see how you grew. Show your process. Be proud of the fact that you started with rough edges and made something sharper, smarter, stronger.

Iteration isn't an admission of failure. It's a declaration of commitment.

It says, "I'm not done getting better."

That's putting the finish on.

The Only Way to Fail Is to Quit

If you're willing to keep improving, you'll find your way.

Not overnight. Not without setbacks. But iteration is a long game strategy, and it works. You just have to stay in it.

Those who finish once are lucky. Those who finish twice are learning. Those who finish over and over again? They become unstoppable.

Because done isn't a destination. It's a discipline.

Action Step

Take one thing you've finished and review it with fresh eyes. Write down three things you'd do differently next time. Then schedule time *this week* to implement those changes. Improvement isn't random. It's a habit.

Edward Beale with William Parry

JAMES DYSON (INVENTOR)

Dyson famously built 5,127 prototypes before his first bagless vacuum cleaner worked. Each failed model taught him something new: better seals, stronger motors, improved cyclonic designs. He didn't hide prototypes; he iterated publicly, refining and relaunching until success. His persistence turned "version 0.0001" into a multi-billion-dollar business. Dyson's saga underscores the final lesson: **finishing is just the beginning - relentless iteration propels work from good to great.**

PIXAR (ANIMATION STUDIO)

When Pixar set out to create *Toy Story* they didn't arrive at a polished script or final storyboard overnight. The team built dozens of rough animated sequences strung together with temporary voices and scratch sound effects. Early cuts felt disjointed: jokes fell flat and pacing lagged. So Pixar's directors and artists held "brain trust" sessions - candid reviews where every reel was critiqued, pinwheeled, and refined to produce fresh versions of key scenes. By embracing that painful, repetitive process of build–test–revise, they transformed *Toy Story* into a cultural phenomenon. Pixar's journey proves the mantra: **finishing a first draft is only the beginning - real excellence emerges through iteration.**

Edward Beale with William Parry

Chapter 11

THE ONLY WAY OUT IS THROUGH

⬇

By now, you've heard the hard truths.

You've faced the resistance. You've seen the mess. You've wrestled with fear, fatigue, money, clutter, shame, and life itself. And through it all, you've also seen what's possible:

Progress. Completion. Clarity. Momentum.

You've learned that "done" isn't handed to anyone - it's claimed, step by step, often in silence, always with effort.

You've read enough. Now it's your turn. Go chase the other side of done.

Go finish.

You don't need to be perfect. You don't need to feel ready. You don't need anyone else's permission. What you need is to act. Today. Even if it's rough. Even if it's small. Especially if it's hard.

Because on the other side of hesitation... is motion. On the other side of fear... is proof. And on the other side of done... is *you*, evolved, refined, celebrated, alive.

On the other side are your Finished Things.

We won't pretend the path is easy. But we can promise it's worth it.

You will become stronger than your distractions. You will outlast the doubt. You will look back one day - quietly, maybe even tearfully - and realize:

"I made it. I didn't give up. And now it's real."

No one can take that from you.

This book isn't the end of something. It's a signal. A call. A small, solid hand on your shoulder reminding you: *You've got this. Keep going.*

And when you do?

You'll find yourself on the other side of done - not just with a finished project, but with this deeper knowledge:

You can do hard things. You can finish what you start, all the way to *done*. And you're only just getting started.

We'll see you on the other side.

- **Ed & Bill**

YOUR NAME HERE (FINISHER)

Here's a page for your finished things.

When (*...when...*) you ship, write the story here. Fill the page with success.

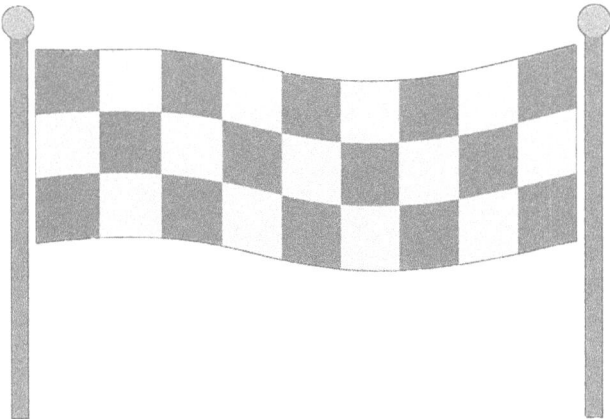

Edward Beale with William Parry

PRAISE FOR FINISHED THINGS

"...in the same category as the One Minute Manager and Chicken Soup for the Soul. Should be required reading for any freshman heading to college...or any executive assuming a new leadership role." – **Don Trone**, *CEO Behavioral Governance Institute; "Father of Fiduciary"*

"...a wisdom-packed field guide to the hardest part of any mission - crossing the finish line. Starting is important, but finishing is transformative." – **Jim Parejko**, *SVP Engineering, Quality, & Test*

"...a hands-on Agile-like approach for completing projects. Set clear goals, deliver consistently, iterate effectively, and embrace progress over perfection - all essential project completion strategies." **Joseph Staier**, *Chief Engineer of Cyber & Networks*

ABOUT THE AUTHORS

Long-time collaborators Ed Beale and Bill Parry have shipped finished things in art, literature, music, theatre, video and audio production, human performance, athletics, learning, aviation, software, manufacturing, sales, marketing, travel, history, corporate management and leadership (among others), and refuse to ever finish chasing the other side of done.

Ed retired from the U.S. Coast Guard as the academic dean of leadership development. He held private sector roles with nPlusOne Group, GP Strategies, Metris Global, and Boston Scientific, where he shipped numerous finished things. A Disney Institute graduate and speaker at leadership, learning, and sales events, Ed works to inspire positive corporate culture.

Bill is a sales and revenue enablement leader with over 30 years of military and corporate experience. His career began with the U.S. Coast Guard where he developed skills in leadership, instructional design, and human performance. After finding a huge disparity between content taught and what sellers actually did, Bill has since focused on shipping sales and team skill development programs that produce real world results.

www.ingramcontent.com/pod-product-compliance
Lightning Source LLC
Chambersburg PA
CBHW062004040426

42447CB00010B/1907